Journeys

Written by Paul Bennett

Wayland

CRISS X CROSS

Bodies   Fairgrounds   Light   Special Days
Boxes   Growth   Patterns   Textures
Changes   Holes   Rubbish   Weather
Colours   Journeys   Senses   Wheels

Picture acknowledgements

The publishers would like to thank the following for allowing their photographs to be reproduced in this book: J. Allan Cash 8, 10 (top), 15, 25 (both); John Cleare/Mountain Camera 27; Bruce Coleman Ltd 18 (Kevin Burchett), 21 (top, Norman Tomalin), 22 (top, Norbert Rosing) (below, Frank Lane), 23 (Frans Lanting), 26 (top, Keith Gunnar); Eye Ubiquitous 28; Sally and Richard Greenhill 4, 5 (top), 14 (below), 19 (top); Tony Stone International 13 (top), 16, 20 (top), 24; Wayland Picture Library 5 (below), 7 (below), 9 (top), 10 (below), 11 (top), 12 (below); ZEFA 6, 7 (top), 9 (below), 11 (below), 12 (top), 13 (below), 14 (top), 17 (both), 20 (below), 26 (below), 28, 29.

Cover photography by Daniel Pangbourne, organized by Zoë Hargreaves. With thanks to The Fox Primary School.

First published in 1993 by
Wayland (Publishers) Ltd
61 Western Road, Hove
East Sussex BN3 1JD, England

Editor: Hazel Songhurst
Designers: Jean and Robert Wheeler

Consultant: Lorraine Harrison is a senior lecturer in Early Years Education Studies for teacher training courses at the University of Brighton. Lorraine has a particular interest in geographical education for children from the ages of 5-12. She wrote the notes for parents and teachers and provided the topic web.

British Library Cataloguing in Publication Data
Bennett, Paul.
Journeys. – (Criss Cross)
I. Title II. Series
910

ISBN 0-7502-0511-3

Typeset by DJS Fotoset Ltd, Brighton, Sussex
Printed and bound in Italy by L.E.G.O. S.p.A., Vicenza

Contents

Walking 4

By road 6

By train 8

Across water 10

Up in the air 12

Moving 14

Pilgrimages 16

Fun journeys 18

Emergency journeys 20

Animal journeys 22

Beneath the sea 24

Up a mountain 26

Into space 28

Notes for parents and teachers 30

Topic web 31

Glossary 32

Index 32

Words printed in **bold** are explained in the glossary on page 32.

Walking

Every day, people make journeys.
They travel to school or work, to the
shops or to the park. Where do you
think these people are going?

We usually make short journeys on foot. The children in this picture are walking home from school. ▶

Walking is a slow way to travel. These people are strolling along a path down to the beach. What arc they enjoying about their walk? ▼

By road

We make journeys every day by road.
These German children have just
finished school. They are running to
catch the bus that will take them
to their homes.

Journeys through towns and cities are often very slow because there is a lot of traffic. On this **motorway** in Canada, cars can travel very fast.

This family is having fun riding bicycles along a quiet road. What are some of the ways you have travelled along a road?

By train

Have you ever been on a journey by train? Many years ago, you would have travelled on a steam train that made a lot of dirty smoke.

Today, many trains run on electricity which makes them travel very fast between towns and cities. Look for the electricity **cables** that stretch above this train.

You can also make journeys on trains that run above or under busy city streets. Here is an overhead railway in Sydney, Australia.

Across water

People make all kinds of journeys in boats. Big ocean liners take tourists on **cruises** all round the world, stopping at different places on the way.

These people have just been for a trip on a lake.

These people are paddling along a fast-flowing river. In a small boat, the journey can be very bumpy if the water is rough.

A hovercraft travels on top of the water on a cushion of air.

Up in the air

Have you ever travelled up in the air? Look at the picture of these hot-air balloons. Before there were aeroplanes some people made journeys by hot-air balloons. Today, people ride in them for fun.

The fastest way to travel is by aeroplane. These children look as if they enjoyed their flight!

The aircraft *Concorde* flies so fast that it can take you across the Atlantic Ocean in just a few hours.

From a hang-glider you have a good view of the countryside below.

Moving

Have you ever moved to a new home? First, you must pack all your **possessions**. A removal truck carries them to your new home.

You must unpack again at your new home and decide where to put all your things.

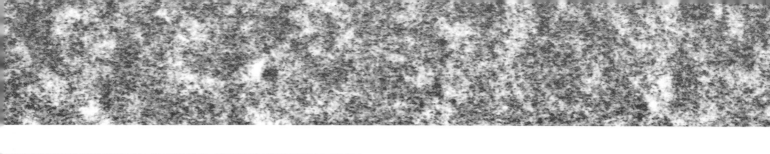

In some countries, **nomads** travel from
place to place with their animals in
search of fresh food and water for them.
They carry all their possessions with them.

Pilgrimages

A pilgrimage is a special journey to a holy place. Many Hindus make a pilgrimage to Varanasi in India to bathe in the River Ganges.

Lourdes in France is visited by many Roman Catholics. They believe the water at Lourdes can cure people of their illnesses.

These Christian **pilgrims** are taking part in a procession in the holy city of Jerusalem in Israel.

Fun Journeys

Some journeys can be great fun! The people on this fairground ride are enjoying flying high in their seats. Have you ever been to a fairground? Which was your favourite ride?

Going on holiday is
fun. The journey is
very exciting.

When you go
camping you
can travel
wherever you like.

Emergency journeys

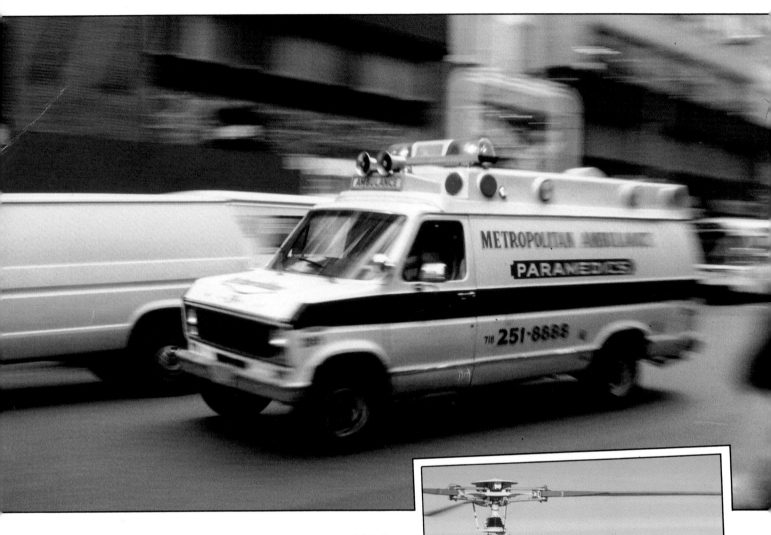

A very sick person will be taken quickly to the hospital by ambulance.

Sometimes, a helicopter may be used to make the emergency journey. ▶

20

A fire engine speeds through the streets to get to a fire. It has flashing lights and a loud **siren**.

This lifeboat is racing to the rescue. Can you think of any other rescue services that save people from danger?

Animal journeys

Many animals make very long journeys called **migrations.** Birds like these geese fly south in the autumn and north in the spring. Do you know why?

Many fish return to the place where they were born in order to lay their eggs. These salmon have travelled across the ocean and must jump up waterfalls to find the part of the river where they were once eggs.

This flock of Monarch butterflies is resting after flying thousands of kilometres from the USA to a forest in Mexico, where they will spend the winter.

Beneath the sea

Divers wear **wetsuits** and carry
aqualungs to explore under the water.
Look at the ink-cloud squirted out by
the octopus. It wants to frighten away
the diver.

These people are travelling inside a **submarine.** They are looking through the windows at the fish and other animals that live beneath the sea.

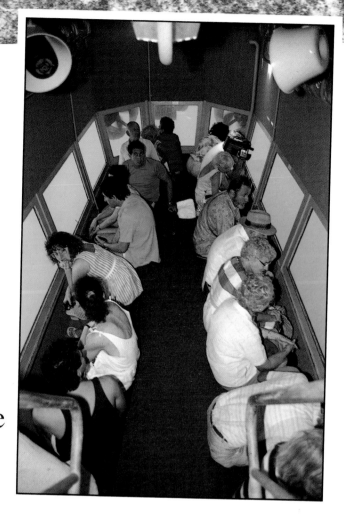

This **submersible** can go deep under the sea where it is very cold and dark. Can you see the light on the front of it?

Up a mountain

The journey to the top of an ice-covered mountain can be hard work and very dangerous. These climbers are roped together so that if one of them falls the other climber can save him.

At the top, the view is often amazing.

This girl is learning to climb up high rocks. When she is older she may want to climb a mountain.

Into space

The Space Shuttle is **launched** into space by giant rocket boosters.

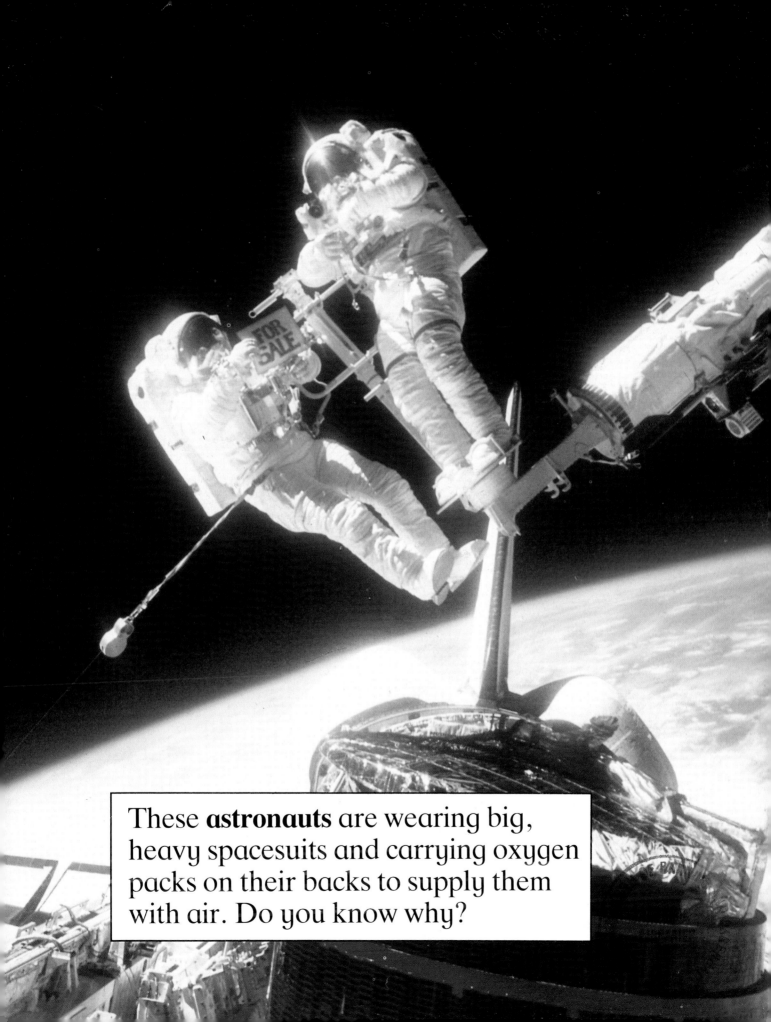

These **astronauts** are wearing big, heavy spacesuits and carrying oxygen packs on their backs to supply them with air. Do you know why?

Notes for parents and teachers

Maths
The ability to sort, classify and record are essential components of mathematical understanding.
- Children can select vehicles according to a simple classificatory system.
- Children can be encouraged to create simple bar charts and frequency tables from the collection of appropriate information.
- Looking at simple timetables can result in the calculation of cost/time/distance of particular journeys.

Language
The topic of journeys creates many opportunities for language development.
- Sharing, listening and talking about appropriate stories is of enormous benefit to children at this age.
- Children can be encouraged to compose a story about a journey which could either be real or imagined.
- Creating a diary linked to a journey or weekend away could be shared with friends.

Science and Technology
Through investigative work, children can discover much scientific understanding. Many of the pictures in the book will provide a stimulus for further work.
- Children could be encouraged to design and make their own transport vehicles. Further investigation into the effects of pushing and pulling could extend this activity.
- Children can explore those factors which make an object float or sink. They can relate their findings to their own experiences.

Geography
- The child's mapping ability can be extended by encouraging the drawing of local routes and comparing them with a simple 'map' of the area.
- Direct experience in the local environment can lead to consideration of road improvements, the place of pedestrian crossings, etc.
- Children can be encouraged to link places with the help of simple maps, or even photographs of an area. In this way, they begin to synthesise and relate ideas connected with the 'wider' world.

History
It is of great interest and fascination for children to find out about life in the past in order to discover and explain change.
- Children could be encouraged to talk to grandparents to find out about the journeys they undertook and types of transport used.
- Using appropriate photographs can provide opportunities for children to talk about and appreciate change over time.
- Learning about people who travelled in the past will add dimension to historical enquiry.

Multicultural
It is important that children have opportunities to appreciate differences and similarities that exist throughout the globe.
- Watching television programmes which focus upon journeys into the 'wider' world can provide children with a realistic image of unfamiliar places and cultures.
- The investigation of religious journeys could extend from those introduced in this text.

Dance/Drama/P.E.
- Children can be encouraged to travel in different ways, as individuals and in groups.
- Allowing children to invent pathways in and around space as well as using simple apparatus is likely to enhance body awareness.
- The creation of collaborative work designed to encourage children to re-create the movements of vehicles can enhance aesthetic quality.

Music
- Children can listen to music associated with particular journeys.
- Creating a musical accompaniment to a poem encourages creativity and free expression.
- Children may enjoy listening to and singing songs from other cultures.

Art/Craft
- Children can observe a variety of photographs/paintings that depict journeys.
- The drawing of an imaginary journey could provide the stimulus for imaginative writing.
- Close observation of material and artefacts associated with journeys could provide the starting point for 2 or 3 dimensional work.

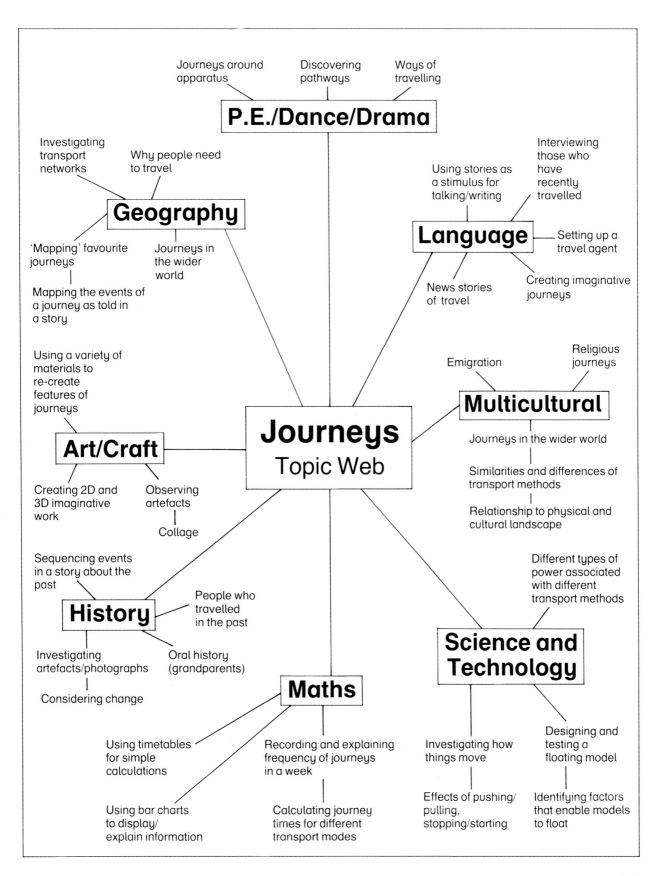

Journeys around apparatus   Discovering pathways   Ways of travelling

P.E./Dance/Drama

Investigating transport networks

Why people need to travel

Geography

'Mapping' favourite journeys

Journeys in the wider world

Mapping the events of a journey as told in a story

Using a variety of materials to re-create features of journeys

Art/Craft

Creating 2D and 3D imaginative work

Observing artefacts

Collage

Journeys
Topic Web

Using stories as a stimulus for talking/writing

Interviewing those who have recently travelled

Language

Setting up a travel agent

News stories of travel

Creating imaginative journeys

Emigration

Religious journeys

Multicultural

Journeys in the wider world

Similarities and differences of transport methods

Relationship to physical and cultural landscape

Different types of power associated with different transport methods

Sequencing events in a story about the past

History

People who travelled in the past

Investigating artefacts/photographs

Oral history (grandparents)

Considering change

Maths

Science and Technology

Using timetables for simple calculations

Recording and explaining frequency of journeys in a week

Investigating how things move

Designing and testing a floating model

Using bar charts to display/ explain information

Calculating journey times for different transport modes

Effects of pushing/ pulling, stopping/starting

Identifying factors that enable models to float

Glossary

Aqualungs Cylinders full of air joined to a long tube and a mask. They are carried by divers so that they can breathe underwater.

Astronauts Space travellers.

Cables Long wires that carry electricity.

Cruises Long sea journeys.

Launched Set off.

Migrations Long journeys made each year by some birds and animals.

Motorway A wide, straight road separated into different lanes where traffic can travel faster than on other roads.

Nomads People who have no fixed home but travel from place to place.

Pilgrims The name given to people who go on a pilgrimage.

Possessions All the things people own.

Sirens Instruments that send out loud warning signals.

Submarine A kind of ship that can travel underwater.

Submersible A small deep-sea submarine.

Wetsuit A close-fitting rubber suit worn by divers to keep them warm underwater.

Index

Aeroplane 12
Astronauts 27, 28
Atlantic Ocean 13

Canada 7
Concorde 13

Divers 24

Emergency vehicles 20, 21

Fairground rides 18

Hang-glider 13
Helicopter 20
Holiday 19
Hot-air balloons 12
Hovercraft 11

Jerusalem 17

Lourdes 17

Mexico 23
Migrating 22, 23
Motorways 7

Nomads 15

Ocean liners 10

Pilgrims 16, 17

Removal truck 14
River Ganges 16

Space Shuttle 28

Traffic 6, 7
Trains 8, 9

Walking 4, 5